THE BLUEST KALI

SCHEREZADE SIOBHAN

LITHIC PRESS
FRUITA, COLORADO

THE BLUEST KALI

Cover art by Ishita Basu Mallik
Layout by Kyle Harvey

THE BLUEST KALI
SCHEREZADE SIOBHAN
ISBN 978-1946-583024
Lithic Press

LITHIC PRESS
fine books for an old planet
www.lithicpress.com

SYNOPSIS

I write to remember my life through its subtle and feral vacancies. As an Indo-Rroma writer, names like mine are subject to anonymity, erasures and/or margins, therefore I also write to un-marginalize, to stomp on the white playground of a page, to leave the ox-black venerations of my psychoses. My writing is unapologetically polyglottal and sometimes refuses to translate itself to a convenient assortment of meanings. I am interested in a feminist psychology that enables neurodivergent women of colour to decipher their mental and environmental habitats.

The Bluest Kali is a series of linguistic exorcisms through the corridors of a brown woman's clinical depression, dissociations and displacements that extend from psychological to spiritual exiles. It invites the ghosts that can't be silenced through pills and psychiatric coda to dance in a naked catharsis. It enters its monstrosities without anchors; it incants its own beheading. This is the unsaying of what is betrayed when the mind locks itself out of the body.

CONTENTS

Part III – Left of Azul

THE BLUEST KALI

Part I : Zubaan (Tongue & Language)

THE MIRROR I WON'T

i

The valley stretches before me like an echo of God
Who amongst us can remain unwounded by this amaranth

strophe of green? The first boy's limbs are tilted lightwood, his
hair is unlit newsprint. His heart was quartered as if a golden apple

We eventually forget him. There are too many bodies to remember
The precise silhouette tailored to the dimming of a blotted lake

All the houses we omit still remain standing like stubborn epitaphs
This is the ethnography of missing teeth. This is a library of stolen fingernails.

This is a lap full of broken birds.   This is the holy asymmetry
Of choked up *chinars* crimsoning tin roofs shrouded in a heresy of smoke

Arms of darkened copper dig through a time-coarsened vernacular
Soon, soft concavities belch and shudder with the gist of a bloody debris

Their mothers will disappear behind veils, low clouds silenced by a murder
of crows. Stilled feathers of black henna filigreeing the reddest horizon

within their hands   Their eyes will finally be emptied of prayers and ghosts
                                    Their bodies frozen into a snow-limned map of a graveyard

ii

All the men lined up in a tessellation of dormant volcanoes.
My sky wore the skin of knifed fish. What doesn't kill you
Deafens you with the same questions on a daily basis—
What is your father's name? What is your job? Why don't you
Have one? Are you carrying a weapon? Are you a terrorist?
I am saw-bladed by a mule's rhetoric. My firstborn was named
Veiled Arson. When they began to hand flamethrowers to those
who had dreams essenced from clay, I heard the horse chestnut flog
our attic's skull with the sadism of a bulletproof soldier. I know my love

for this land is at best a myth, at worst—a slur. Even then, this mud is
what spat me out like a common flea. This riverbed galvanized the torque
in my wings. In a language I am thawed from, a single word stands for both—
tongue and language. *Zubaan. Ya'allah,* I am already fossil, a yellowing flank
planted in a desert of mayflies. All around me raindrops skip like drugged
white spiders loosened from a heavenly cupboard. God occupies me as
a shapeless hunger. A million forgeries to articulate the simple loss of each limb.
The elm of my spine was sedated, abridged to obedience. I can tuck the pin
Of a grenade between my teeth like a scared animal picking its blind infant.
I am begging to the ones whose bootprints lick my back like tire tracks in
a graying snow— Tell me when did the weight strapped
to my chest decide to spell itself as a bomb instead of a child?

Aberrata/ Unmapped – I

in the library, i am teething on a coffee table book
about the jackhammered brothels of leningrad. all the tin
gods and straw dolls. puppets gutted to their ceramic bones.
next to me three middle-aged mexican students memorize
the newest echelons of the periodic table. ask me
to pronounce radioactive. i whisper: stepfather.

his hand is on my thigh and my throat is full of red sea.
the science of volcanoes is blueprinted in the stomach.
today, his blood won't clot in a river of molasses.
today, the basa fillet sizzled in lemongrass and cumin
like my ice-nuzzled cheek under his seething palm.

my slit is sorrow. his length is knife.
i stain his sheets. he prays between my thighs.

when the blood dries, it turns to the colour of my race.
white linen like saltwater. my mottling reminiscent of thumb-
pressed cocoa. the first time is fear. all the other times - forgetting.

at the poetry performance, someone sings - we are all one earthquake
away from being unwanted. refugees.
at the airport they ask - what is your middle name?
we halt and chew - second generation.

my body is a sequence of stigmata.
my heart is unpronounceable.

at angeline, the iraqi poet speaks of the hunger under the head-scarf.
on the tv 5 ex-jurors wear bands in support of a 14 year old who shot
a 12 year old coz boys shouldn't wear green prom dresses or high heels.
at the clinic, a transwoman shows me 6 stitches sleeping on her upper lip -
baby snake quivering in the sands. *i was just trying to walk home.*

i was just trying.

fuck those poems about fog and orchids.
fuck the portraits of lavender snow.

if there is something to say
i'd rather it be as hard
and as violent
as the world whose burning window
i am.

Aberrata/ Unmapped – II

What is the temperature in Providence right now? Skateboarder with the shiva-blue tattoo and a notebook solved et coagula. It is hard to undo the grayness from the tongue of this cold weather. It is hard to blossom wings out of a shadow. This time I remembered your birthday, didn't I? Water sign; the river turning into an ossuary of snakes. I am sorry we have come to be such widening absences to each other. I am reading a poem by Zaffar Kunial and that infallible blue jazz trumpeting behind *"Now we separate. / for the first time."* Along the beach, I found a canary yellow rock hibernating inside the wet hollow of driftwood as if the seaweed had laid a secret egg.

x

Today I am menstrual and untouched : an errored autumn of atavisms. But it is winter where we are. Where we left ourselves be. Where your *Moab* corresponds to my *Yamuna*. The sky won't speak to the oaks anymore; all the clouds are gathered in a salmon pink cockscomb - the throat of thunder slowly bleached into a disappearing light. Once upon a time, our bodies stretched out against each other like tightropes meant for red-mud *malkhamb* gymnasts. Once upon a time our bodies weren't afraid of the taut truth; a long room full of nocturnal insects dithering on the dry, dark marble. Everything I am saying to anyone is an act of describing a house from the inside as someone takes a wrecking ball to it.

x

Hello, weird dirt heart. Hello, blackbird elegies. Hello, Time We Never Had. On 22nd when I write back, it is a graveyard kicking itself out from under a singing cathedral. *Subject Line: Help me! I think I am going to kill myself!* I know of that precise low in the ellipse of depression where all the feathers have fled the bone, where the skin is only alive with the sense of maggots. I write to you when skeletal and burning. Not for rebirth but for epitaph. Only you could care enough to throw a rose in the shower of soil drizzling over my uncoffined departure. And you do. Again and again.

x

This hurts more. Everything that has died inside me returns in an epiphany of ghosts. I am conditioned to be most pleasant to those whom I hate most. I nod and nod and nod as if that can eclipse the blasphemy of their shared histories or cure her verbal diarrhea. When I tell you, I am doing well all I mean is I want to quit myself without an aftermath.

x

Next : I want to go back to the place I erased with my own footsteps

relapse

The only possible return is inward, not backward.

(a fragment from Gustavo Pérez-Firmat's diary)

let us begin by blessing the mouth as its own massacre.
let us say i as girl am a hysterics of continuance

when continuance is bilked dry, is unwelcomed.
this blood i skulk is a river of glass wool -

whoever is touched is tendered into an arson.
in the psych ward, i am pigeonholing the vestiges

of a memory widened on the stirrups of DSM.
there are two kinds of remembrance - procedural

and volatile. i have watched women turn into lightning
rods - splintered auguries unwavered by brute force

of a scientific noumena. women limned in blue copperas,
misshapen waters - an oeuvre of bulletproof coda you can't

dismember with your blunt thrusts. here is a diagram for how
the brain occults its collapsing flames. here is the medicine

hissing more omen than any injury. i come to dig my own
cadaver exquisito from the whittling of these night-wounded

agoras. i come to sleep amidst a mise-en-scène of traumas
too ample to ever be absent. joy should be more than mere

compensation for muting your scars, should be more
than a succession of lacks deciding how the body can be

disclosed.   Or where.

Remission

To get better does not mean it goes away.
No. It means you have finally learned how
to jamb a fist in the pacifist. Learned to digest
before it devours. Supersonic. Metabolic.
This browser-hatched brainstorm. To write,
to wreck, to retch, to requiem – the cortex
and vent; the sap of each syllable. To say,
suleiman; you are a dagger dancing on my
jugular. Each cell is coronated as carousel
of something tectonic. Something detonating
its headwound against the hospital bed. I,
hemorrhage in rabbit-sized lily ponds. Some
-thing flint-toothed is scratching at the ratchet
of a red-roomed stupor. When can we start looking
for survivors instead of heroes? Here, this body.
Hear, this body. Its electric blanket. Its box guitar.
Its scissored chords. I am 13 different kinds of
amnesia. All busted lips. A barstool turned crystal
-ball. A decade of curs locked up behind my eyes.
The technique sharpens its occam's razor on your
fingers. The technique is to lie down and pretend as
if you were lifeless. The technique is a paradox.
Self to save or spend. This. I don't need to pretend.

Fragments on MDD*

Post the electric fugue, the body returns as a corvus shadow - nickel thumbprints of stars pushing in the vortex of a November black - tongue coiled dark. *Hymn & howl.*

Is sadness an illness?

When the temperature cocks its trigger, the mercury jumps with its rabbit-knees. I could swallow all the silver fevering the steel. I could tell you of the way the sorrow slithers through each tissue in a reptilian noose.

I am an apostle of science. I am also its rodent labyrinth, its lip-synching crash test dummy. Magnetic prongs nettle me to a red hypnosis. I am rope burn and blue suede. An ignition through the textile of persona.

I am alive in the conflagrations of this psychosis / a purring silhouette of silk / sheared by a tinder-tongued deja vu.

Let's play hangman, says the spiralbound memento. Let's incant the dramaturgy. Let's push a storm of placebo down the brittle champagne flute of your trachea. Let's kiss each medicine cabinet on its unlocked mouth.

From this angle, the floor looks like a fibrous infection. It's limp grey is loudly contaminated. This is the architecture of an amygdala hijack. Teeth dug into the tapestry of the afghan, nails crafting little roses of anemic blood into the ashen oasis.

I am part ghost, part lighthouse, the darling glow of fuck-you gold. You are paltry in your coarse brass. You can keep barking your flat spleen. You came from an anatomy of rabid mouths, a gangling ego - a zealotry of those who are atlas-bound to the karma of a second brain weeping like a phantom limb.

Gladly, the experiment. Gladly the bastard courage of a fatherless daughter. Gladly, the hot needle, the ripe lemon; the earlobe blotted to ruby dust. The sharp treble juliennes each nerve. Skin now jeweled in the twin moons of grandmother's pearls. Something has to be split for something else to gush and shine.

Love begins as a single room. Love grows into a whole house. As much shoved to forget in the basement as in the attic. Heartache stacked like a broken stepladder. Tutored amnesia thickening the dust on each photograph.

We are a tilt of vine, sheaves of jade - I find your green pulse. My eye is tender to your small flame.

And yet, all cutting is not harvest.

The mind with its weather of a stockholmed Persephone.

When the heart has been robbed, every word sharpens itself to a weapon.

I offer you the myth of forgetting. Under the bed rocking itself into a secret exorcism.

I ask - Can I unoccur? And so you devour me to the aura of my bones. The skull fucked into an entropy of calypso moths.

Today I didn't hurt. Enough.

Today I did enough. Hurt

MDD : Major Depressive Disorder

Rx DSM

Age interrogates the refugee / ghosts buried in my bones
Consider genealogy / Consider the codes corseting the capsules
Consider this beautiful bomb ticking / at the wormhole in my skull

The center doesn't blur / me (anymore) / I trust
the impermanence of strangeness. / O memory, mother of mine –
you came light as sparrowwings / heavy as an elephant's bloated carcass
Through the flotsam, this rough wave of my rising, / sometimes
I escalate without shape – more smoke than song

A dream drills itself into the wetness of my brain. A precise intimacy
entering me like a trepanation. Consider these bodies mapped from
the *saudade* of a thousand burning roses. You drizzle anti-depressants.
You say a lifelong childhood. You array pills in pages full of dirty taxonomy.
You beat the molten gold into the sanguine iron of blackout cages.
I pet the animal through its bloodlust and gangrene.

I came here to unmap myself; to be galvanic
between diamonds and doldrums. I want to be something
beyond the pale gasp of comprehension; something
that demands hemorrhaging flashlights, helicopters hooting
at snowed pinnacles – a Smith-Rock anarchy of nomadic birds of prey.

The light you made wasn't always clean or safe.
Often, you peeled the plastic off the wired synapse,
a wild temperature drugging the vertebrae.
Sometimes you were bright - naked and fatal,
a single line of voltage slithering through deep, deep waters.

I was possessed by a language / as unfinished / as the depression of desire.

Consider it an addiction to tenderness.
Consider it the elegiac spine of a porcelain berry vine -
the blackish purple of each bruise. / Mouthfuls of dark fruit.

My battery is at 15% on America's loneliest highway

All morning we have been trying to language a loss
speeding out in ambulance howls and the muezzin's contralto

Let us be known in the shape of bell jars
that are hatching the first firmament of swallowtails

I can speak but only as a prelude / to a serration

It is true that a crow has no other name but that of a crow
Take these words - the hexed locus of each skipped stone
eclipsing the kaleidoscopic rivers of my grandmother's lac bangles

English is clinical. Urdu is karmic

If you open the box then a body with its veins torched black

A mosaic of psychopomp
An unapologetic rattling
A spider sexed in amber

Against the ontology of bed linen, a rapid argument
with theorems of knuckled moans. Sleep is an ache

I can't body or ghost. Any nostalgia is alms
for unfolding a mind disembodied in deus ex machine

Still we measure the consummation of years
thumbing an index of frugal keepsakes

Here is a forgetting how the wind imitates
my grandfather's coughing steps

Here is a newness a 12 year old asking me
how do people who come back from a coma remember
which body is theirs

Nafs (Pulse)

All night I wait for language to form me.
— Alejandra Pizarnik, "L'obscurité des eaux" trans. Cecilia Rossi

I receive God faintly. In the asemic warp of traffic lights.
In the failed kintsugi of ceramic plates, the wirebasket
of his chest where blood collocates like perfumed pinecones.
It is easy to forget the story within the body, to become air -
an invisible witness. Each death divining the shorn wings of
my mothertongue.

x

In a dream your white shirt hangs on the arm of a redwood.
It is both: a ghost and a flag. You descend into my premonitions
like a cinnabar moth. Your wings maculated, mapped - freshly
uncocooned. I study the brevity of your dimensions, your scale
of survival. Stroke you to a thin tremble. Angle you in an artful
entomology. I carom your sacred winging. Slowly pin you
down by the disappearance of your uncontested peripheries.

x

Each waking is a blush of lust, a blast of lush binge, a bender
to la dolce vita. I sleep with No. I kiss its swollen heat.

I swallow its small fist. I let it fill my mouth with a blue cadaver.
Sin with its skin of mink, the copperhead's tongue tickling my ear.

Cunt, an opium bowl, a trickle of plum wine, a bruised blooming.
And you, houndteeth primed for beheadings. My fiend, my still

-to-milk gluttony. Here is your hunter's nose horning the deer's
navel. Here is the spooling Tethys - ancient phosphor,
abuttals of blaze.

Here is a wetness so citrus with its holy flood hypnosis.
Here is my body shrunk into a river-long shudder of prayer.

Sifar

How I faltered into your luminescence corrupting the midnight waters! To swim moonwards was a separate warfare between me and the trellis of nerves soldiering your skin.

+

My body's tilted abecedary, it's primal mezzotint. The risen only speak in tongues of roses and wolves.

+

Spin my silk from the dark folio of crow-scooped saltpans. The oil lamps rephrased in the *qasida* of dark doves.

+

Somewhere else, the storm collared the houses, shook the groves of hunter's green into its own mosaic of liquid gold. Somewhere, a buffalo limped ahead of lightning's ruthless telepathy.

+

I remember my mother shuttering all the windows, unplugging electronics away from their glittering tensions. Our home slowly closing in on me like the tobacco-rotted brownyellow whorl of His mouth.

+

I want to say I love You, but instead this photograph of *dasht-e-margo* - hillspeech cognitions of terra-cotta, a hawk descending upon the stone like a blind archangel.

+

From distance, I swallow the rain down to its slowest blade and still can't tell if I am the thinned silver of God's fallen tongue or its bloody song.

Part II : Mira as Kali

In Other Trees, Other Songs

when i was 8 or 9 my stepfather tried to hang me when he could not abuse me anymore. blue nylon rope. mango tree. i flailed like a still alive fish being gutted slowly.

yesterday facebook asked me (again) if i knew this man. if i wanted to add him as a friend. i stepped onto the cold marble of our basil and tomato decorated terrace and remotely assessed all the swaying clotheslines, trying to guess which had a blue nylon rope underneath.

i watch the coconut seller hack at the fruit's stubborn green head like a practiced butcher till we can peek into its *malai* flesh. is this how pain whets us, tenders us – fissures us to our soft visceral rhizome of undoing?

someone you love leaves a keyhole open in your eye. the sands of time slowly pouring out as saltwater and aphasia. you think of the wheat grains tottering out of a mouse-gnawed gunny sack. the body leaving through the body.

the heart is a brief cry of an animal meeting the music of a falling blade.

i want to live elsewhere. a place where new isn't always now.

i am tired of being awake. i am tired of eyelids and doorbells. i am tired of sunlight entering my bed like a cheating husband.

at the parking lot, he says – the greater medicine is to not want happiness but remain in the snug arms of a neutral nothingness. 3 years later, i am in agreement right down to the tip of each toe.
early morning as i wait for the car to take me to the airport, in the streets, my nightmare walks in the form of a woman with motel carpet hair howling profanities at the morning joggers. she screams snippets from a rape. the psychosis as stark as a throbbing nerve.

someone's grandfather who sits in the temple garden and for whom i buy a bag of toffee every saturday. his son locks him out between 10 am and 6 pm. he shows me a picture of his dead wife and tells me how he'd courted her in a game of kite-flying.

to be loved like a fir falling to lightning.

when i pray, i ask for a repetition of beginnings. for the strength to forget what i couldn't forgive.

now the numbness is turning into temporary paralysis. this afternoon my lower body remained motionless for 2 hours and i thought of an old folklore where two sisters are given a magical brew and whoever drinks it, turns into a flowering tree for a day. by the end of it, the tree is axed down by a logger, leaving the younger sister with the half girl, half tree torso of the older sister. i am my own sister. i am my own declining forest.

somedays i dream to be as boring and normal as a bowl of breakfast cereal, traffic lights at 8 am, a railway timetable, a desire to be needed.

my grandmother : stained glass lanterns in the living room, orange peel drying in the windowsill, tanjore paintings above my bedpost, rubbing lime juice over the calligraphy of henna on hands, the ears of two earthen lamps tucked into each other till one was full of the darkest kohl. the sparrow who came and stayed in my room the whole night i was shaped into a seashell, my limbs turning into inverted commas on the purple afghan. three years after her death.

i think about the poised arrows of your angled knees. when we meet, the peak of your nose disappears behind the black crayon cirrhus of my hair. our own fledgling earth science; our own hagiography of kisses like quasars.

the friend you miss. the one who is in providence. the one who taught you that it was possible to go to sleep without crying first. the softspoken skateboarder. zero and sigils. the one who is happy and invisible now.

tell me there is more to dreaming than just this never-ending failure of a more absolute death.

airport sutra

it is always the gum-black drop   of my eyebrows -   afghan
hawkmoth crushed   in vine charcoal   a line pilfered from
forough's ash-limned chant   *then*, the troubled wonder
of skin it's feathered undertows   i can aura the guesswork
of their eyes - that blink and slur - *is she one of them, theirs, they*
hers? quarantine is   a home papered in blue   fiction, ripped
teeth of macadam   night-sorrowed jasmines   a leaf of *vark*
ironing it's plenty over the *barfi*   the *khansama* soaking almonds
for rice puddings. *qabbani's* arbor between pewter and teakwood
memory is the worst disease   say *inshallah* and the healing is
hot wax trying to fuse two apologies into a single bone.   *dear*
ghalib, i too am the report of my own fracture. if she were alive
my grandmother would ask of me   a dire grace   would ask
i grow my hair to rival the dark   knotted length of our Time
ask that the heart best be worn   as an amulet wrapped
in a language   i still can't read   but sing more and more of
with each   passing death

Raga

every morning the temples wash their courtyards with the astringent of a cymbal-wail. holy sirens blatting for the release of kidnapped gods. these ears are conch-caves, buried bells for the missing. this is a homegrown hunch, a debatable heuristic, a placard for the happenstance. this is a hope that god even if blind, is not deaf.

x

on the wall raised against my head - a portrait traced in *madhubani*. lord Krishna and his consorts playing beneath a monarchy of gods. beneath them, i - draped in jacquard-woven silk. my lap snugged in ancestral velvet. a cradle for the nest egg. horizontal as a grindstone i pestle my girlhood into. girl. sacred. earthbound. ore. jewel. root. grave.

x

i have inherited a violent cough and an engagement ring. also Salgado's sepia snapshots. the room is a diorama of brittle ice sinking sotto voce in a tall glass of lemonade sherbet. the streets are plastered with posters about summer's en route circus making trapezes out of tree-branches, clotheslines, adolescent arms.

x

i claim solidarity with crows. parade undressed in a somnabulist's fugue. lay open a seduction as spurious as the superficial wounds i dig into my teen¬age knees. my wrists snap rubies. all my dreams bark naked, barbaric hav¬ing lost their costumes in the auctioned theater of your civilized country.

x

your winter-husked city is a church full of provocateurs. every prophet. every nihilist. i collect them all. wash ash off each forehead, set lamps in their ruins; tend to their ghosts as if they were my own orphans.

x

the book asks that widows wear white and don't eat at our table. so the piss-colored porridge is poured into old brass bowls outside the kitchen, next to the heap of sweetmeat wrappings and trampled marigolds. as the night slaps the banyans with a whip made of languor tails, i watch her slowly turn from woman to ghost – the torn, bleached flag of her saree swaying bleakly behind the leaves. nothing fulfills the shell of an afterward. the way light is lowered in a tiger-infested forest. torrid at first, then, spectral; cold and unheard. then, the swift spear of a loud scream cutting through the thicket's chest.

x

the way i entered his bed wearing nothing but anklets so he could relearn me by another sense. i came to him as sound before speech. a song that ascends from music to mourning.

Mira writes about The Mountaineer

There are theoretical expositions, and then there
are visceral actualities.
— Ahmed Salman

Confession that we are a crowning blow of chemicals - this neural or
natural or neutered nuisance of intuition we can't rewire to correspond.

I altar him as an exorcism of infinites.
A lunar mare of bone char and *jahili* odes.

Still his mouth swells in a tidal motion of foreign tongues.
Still his veins remain knotted in a seeding alphabet.

Dusk is a word that exhumes itself from a sanguine dot. *Hardened*
hemoglobin with its final clot in the gut of his borderline

disorder. Every descent begins
with a desire to bend the throttle.

And now he is nothing but a surrogate of innate mud -
a dateless invisibility, loosened fruit in a forever kingdom.

Or perhaps, an ambiguous parasite choking the earshot.
A recurring saltwater force majeure we often ricochet against.

At length, its censure - as intestinal as
a feat of centipedes stroked into a sigil of star-maps.

In the heat of his rugged zealotry is something I can't
unfold enough to fit inside of. So I evanesce as if snow.

Each of our men come with an oystercatchers' grasp, a rattling crate
hunkered beneath the obloquy of sodden depths. A room crushed

to dirt in the very hands of its mason. On a mattress of ash, his insomnia warbles
- your voice, the color of chestnut and riptide, the color of leather harness and stout beer.

The American masochism climaxing slowly within the italics of his eyebrows.
That larval arch is a brief foreclosure of time - an omega

articulated in the tumor of a butte. He knows how to pilgrim
upwards of any timeworn impossibility but always fails

to calculate the speed at which every horizon disappears.

Mira explains *halal/haram*

As dead as some constellations, we perambulate the rotten axis of grit-toothed meatmarkets. Sizzled flesh flattens each street with its lax striation of butcheries kneeling ear-deep in the choppy purr of Cantonese radio. Night is detonated basalt, stained fur - a skyfull of opal-beaked birds embossing the powerline. Here, I perform a visage and incant the body back to its practiced haggle. The length of him is a running voltage slowly corroding the cathodes of my limbs. Appearance: willows hooked in nascent ligature, tonsured pavements; the intimacy of forged displacements. Any kind of gutting is a punctual repositioning of an animal's stamina to exist inside its own vulnerability. A blade partitions my rattleboned gluttony, unlocks the coda of a bloody cartilage. What is the difference between a good surgeon and a good butcher except an economy of bloodlust? In my oily back pocket, you are nothing but jangled metal. I split the coin through its conjoined chiaroscuro. I grey the muscle, daunt the feathers, foil the tendons. Entrust me with the selenography of your tusk-white carcass, your bones embroidered inside an iced fish slanted like a silvered candlestick - I will swallow this bottled fire. I will spit out an oyster of light.

In the small country of snow owls -

we have learned to share our ghosts; a moon dripping its coconut milk anemia, the iridium of bottled bone marrow, a cemetery of half-buried baby teeth.

the crows knit their wings into a sailcloth and the once platinum sky is now a purple iris turning darker than the bitumen black of my depression. the aglo-hungarian is reading to me in spanish. a song of salt and scars. his sun in the water is the single floating bead of a torn tibetan rosary.

seed & perdition. come adrift. come, float & hover.

this is not easy. i am thinking of the pellicle of blood rusting at the root of this thumb. i am thinking about rice and eggs. i am thinking of a lake turning into a junkyard of cars crushed into brittle coins. i am thinking of the distance between exorcism and evacuation – a room i can un-enter. a room that can unlock me.

on the phone, i can hear footsteps chanting above your head in their glottal parroting of a hurricane. i want you to sleep. you just want me.

in sleep, we want each other. in sleep of other is a want. as anonymous as a war orphan.

any day with you is flawlessly ambidextrous. a miracle child picked up and taken to an observatory. a prodigy of stumbling pawns. a child made of prognosis and prescription pills.

the amerik trying to learn my name in his slug-speech. my name is a rhizome for zahir. my name is the kind of grace that takes light to folded corners of a cold mouth. my name is ciudad de las rosas olvidadas. my name is green with the psychology of petals. my name is how your whole body shudders like a loud book under the library's colonial fan.

i am wearing you through the night; a wedding dress with a missing zipper. ivory lace cutting its lip on red wine. wet, coming apart.

oh yes, the havoc of these chintzy fogs. your mind turns radioactive with the colour of chimeras. an atomic furnace. an abandoned factory where they set up kangaroo courts. the sunburned skin of walls smudged with solar lentigo.
in therapy i recognize that any medicine is always grey with the filth of

facelessness. the disease is always the pale pink sunset of a teenage romance.

let me remind you who you were before the violence, before the deer with its heart still warm amid the grains. your hands of brahma. you have made enough streets into beds. this you, this particle of god, this museum of muscle and myth. come, be again.

montserrat or maine or a himalayan basecamp. a tea terrace in darjeeling. i am kissing you as men with safety helmets are dangled into coal shafts. there will be no forgetting how dust swirled in the mountain air like an animal's scent. there will be no fear of hunger or home.

this is the world between us – pregnant with gravity; emptied and beginning.

genres of prey

i am a diabetic who hasn't eaten for 10 hours. it is a transfusion of numbness like carbon monoxide nuzzling each skinny nerve.

in an afternoon asphyxiating on its own sinuses, i am wooing the mongrels sleeping in each of my finger-bones; each drugged cur, all the canker and cuss.

the body can become a cannibal to itself. eat each organ with a gourmet splendour.

the stomach opens up like a venus flytrap – catholic in its welcome; appetite is the distance between ache and amen.

half my lineage haunts me with its orthodox hymnals. here are the raven-feathered words – a row of roma gypsy women; mantilla and cigarrillo. andalusian hands poised with the javelin of a golden cross.

on the entresol of a thigh, i riddle a safety pin to test the failure of feeling. no rats marooned in this goose grass. no friction in the crinoline.

my blood has been hushed into a blackout.

this year, i forgot my father's death anniversary. my god is two decades of guilt. there is no right way to remember so i droop my inklings in an underbelly of fugue states.

love leaves me open like a hammer punishing a stubborn crabshell. how do you convince yourself that all these broken dice, all this dulcitude, this split-sweet meat will find a mouth to melt into?

who can question the authenticity of pain? who can debate these darkrooms, this body trembling in a bathtub like a crimsoned tapir?

i know there are pastel dusks. i know this when my ear reads the air for its radio silence.

in an aeonian nightmare, i struggle with losing my toes. i already miss digging them into the *café au lait* drag of bombay's matte sand. i caved for water. i undid the eruptions, the anchors, the insolvency.

i hunt for untranslatable phrases in my native languages so i can tell you something about love and language.

urdu has many different ways to pronounce loss -

the room grows warm with my fever; i am kiln, i am brick. a cut apple sent to rust. only clay and bone.

from a train, i see a colony of conifers speaking to me in a deft sign language. each tree is as a glossarist. i can sense the wind, now mute with meaning.

to write in english feels like dancing on landmines. at any point, my limbs will rant their straits like a flicker of confetti.

today i felt microscopic; so diminutive that anything could trample me without regret.

home but no direct flights. home but doesn't dot itself on a google map. home but the moth-eaten arthritis of a beautiful pergola. home but a fistful of placebo. home but everyone is gone. home but keep on walking into the river.

depression is a long game of hide and seek where you hid in the attic and they quickly sold the house.

a schizophrenic once told me – i had no one to go to so i made enough people out of myself and now i never run out of togetherness. and then we say fractured, flawed, full – as if there were a key to open the many rooms of loneliness.

his diagnosis is information not knowledge. how many times do i need to apologize for wanting to cradle the wet, wounded bodies of small birds?

we've come here. we must want something. what?

to be readied without hurry. / to be hoped into. / to be hungered for.

genres of grief

this is a catalan state of mind. this is an exodus of roses. this is a motley kindred of phoenixes lulled inside icebergs.

heart is a soundproofed slaughterhouse.

mahler's 9th symphony backslashing the menagerie of your baptisms through chemotherapy a checklist of "i am awake but not alive" on a loop.

the last good night typewritten inside the scuttled gunfire.
the last good night typewritten inside the scuttled gunfire.

a staircase pleating its origami within your spine.

a sparrow-boned venetian statue cracking its torso 's eggshell alabaster to nest a choir of red ants.

your name can only be spelled in a calligraphy of braille on sand.

days you lunged your limbs through windshields of parked cars like a pint-sized, homespun bomb lobbed at a full friday mosque in some anonymous city.

an unopened box of crayons that survives the plane crash.

the pinewood photo frame buried beneath a row of picayune azaleas whispering in lamp-lit undertones.

a month as mauve as your elbows.

a month spiked as a single stiletto hanging haphazard from the railing of an abandoned hotel's balcony.

his and her burial plots.

summer that sweltered the last of weeping willows' tears.

he has eyes like a cognac sunrise.

your father's freshly starched shirt 3 weeks after the funeral.

the continents birthed inside your mother's stretch marks.

hope threshed to a burning shroud.

8-18 is a requiem of silent rage, thereon all music tautening my muscle trembled to a raging.

silence : a blueprint footloose in clay; the years are a crate of blueberries mauled to mulch.

a ruby dress that puts the terror of fallen angels back inside the hearts of men.

an ocean mewing the memory of its swallowed ships.

a dog with irises like frozen opals.

you pattern your dire prayers as a small colony of crop circles god, in turn, was always a flightless bird.

genres of reincarnation

i have been trying to helm your arteries as if a wayfarer woolgathering through the sardined tokyo subway routes.
i have snorted the kanji off the city layout. i am a walking wound raw as fine sashimi.
i am full of regrets pronounced in a foreign language.
i shuttle freight trains battered as a drunk supernova.
i tap train doors when my chink in the armor is a cracked touchscreen that will trespass my catharsis.
i tell you i am rigged like magnum; you are low on ammo and not ready for this.
we have crocheted cobwebs from frayed power lines fluctuating inside our hysteria.
we are the reincarnated Us in ruckus.
we have rung out the bodhran in the soles of our feet as a ballistics simpatico. our heads august before the shooting squad; twin hooded falcons ascending to the coliseum.
i have loved you like a convoy of spotted hyenas mousetrapping a handicapped gazelle.
i have loved you like an allergic kid wadding his mouth with a troop of tamarind before the nosebleed sets in.
i am the the praying mantis slanted on the searchlight. i have waited with an insect's instinct.
this sentiment is diaphanous as a rumor; as opaque as politics.
i have crippled the acoustics of the grottoes shunted against my voicebox.
i am tristessa, paraphrased in your hallelujahs.
i have smutted the madonna half and half in backrooms and billboards.
i have exorcised the revolution from the width of my jargon. you have plaited the ghost of my guerrillas into your corn-rows.
this moment is a whir in crinoline.
this moment is claw mark in the vinyl.
this moment is a hint of hashish smuggled over afghan toll-roads.
your mind is a naked mattress lunged to a shire of cacti and offal, scraping the flashbacks of every body that hulked bedfast and anonymous on its dog-tired canvas.
you are the acid hazmat. you are the photograph of an aftermath; the nuclear idiom sprouting its own chernobyl.
you are my jeopardy topsy turvy like a centaur sleeping inside a cave bat.
i am a telescoped sorcery visible only in the fiasco of shivering rear-view mirrors and weakened french blinds.

you kiss her as though leaving a fake signature on a guest register at a wake. gatecrashing the last rites.
how to touch a girl : an egyptologist deciphering the hieroglyphs that haunt an interred monolith.
the rain falls. an orchestra of balisong. i pocket its length on my tongue's tip till my mouth is a bag of butterfly knives.
when you pronounce my name, it smells like a book laved in petrichor spread over frankincense.
some people are the texture of sandpaper scrubbed with heartache.
my heart is an unmarked gravestone. you are the sleepy eyelid of a single peony petting the stele.

Sundays at Red Room

When he speaks of suicide, I think about the first time we went
for karaoke. That whole trick of goading the rooster out of its coop.

I remember the cheap ceramic silken with poached duck.
The wild instrument of his vodka-fondled voice.

I watched him float away from the derogation of a life
swallowed by rote. Its mulish nerve. Its still-not-strangled syncope.

Soon, he is a room thumping beneath the evanescence
of its own echo. He mouths the lyrics as if he can barter

the defeats of the day against a single hour of loud imagination.
On the lax tapestry, the peanuts come unhusked

like snail shells in a rain of salt. Our skins are shed,
our hollows slick inside this brilliant translucence,

a dulcet stupor. His song is a wayward wish – a thing
unfathered, a groove limned with temporary amnesia.

He knows he can't regret what he forgets
which is almost everything except the music.

The way it hunkers in the marrow of memory,
The way it nudges its teeth into the filthiest vein.

A god rises inside of him – a primitive defiance,
a phantom of insomnia he can void into –

When it was over, we stumbled home
through alleys darker than opioid withdrawals.

Our elbows are curved into treble clefs.
For a while he doesn't speak

in a language of spectral bridges. For a while
his mouth doesn't round itself into a pale noose.

Part III : Left of Azul

totems for desi girls

we were born into a brass plate full of liturgy —tiny hymns
of cow *ghee,* camphor orbs, ears belled after coral hibiscus.

every movement was knotted to an instruction:
today do not thud the ooze of any acid-bellied lemons.

shirk the siren-song of scarlet-lipped chilies. circumvent
ladders. unpet the ebony fur of every athletic cat darting

through your suburban adolescence like a drunk cop's bull
-et. *brown girlhood* is a deftly sharpened modus operandi

to sap the dawning of fate. conch-shell tenets of Saturday evening
palmists combing through the ivory dust of our dead grandmothers

our will tethered to bovine musculatures. their timeworn sacs
pregnant with phylactery. our middle-class mothers cramming

our middle -class mouths with chants excavated from
the groins of jaundiced prayer books. anything

to stall our dowry deaths, *sarees* burning like flags
of bombed countries. *anything.* to avoid dragging

our bodies through the cooling tar like a steel pipe.
to not make a dollhouse from our own cutglass ribcages.

to forget that our bodies were both—talisman and prison.

log #4

the tree we anchor turns into a kurdish folksong.
valleys of coral snakes and ochre moons swelling into holy bread -

earth kneaded into domes and dunes -
its water glimmering with the prayer of gravity.

do the rivers dream of dilaudid?
does the child know of the distance
between   the voice and the body ?

once on a phonecall, i performed an abstraction of ropes.
our third invention. our memory knotted into black braids.

it is said that girls are taught to apologize
for every path they can or can't take.

the mountain comes unconditioned
of it gender. the dust with its tiny mouth

will swallow each oval of velocity.
will touch everything. will hold nothing.

a girl is told she is nothing. she hums
into the soft dark - just wait,

till i come back
and eat you bare.

till your heart cries blue.
till your bones are fear

Tilth

Proud of vein, he is how the earth spires its
forests. My body, his new bower of umbels.

A woman in the prism. Antares, foxfire.
My botched afterglow. His tongue, the gilt

of mud-scented leafhoppers. I remember
the time he said his heart had gone from

red to purple; a clutch of saskatoon chatoyant
in vices of the most Russian violets—his *wajood's*

cold tarring is what I yearned to a cut. All our birds
duskworn to sequin his calico to a centauresque.

To fly in shivers. The snow, lambent, sotto voce. All
of its white keeping my bones icicled in his long ache.

after cordoba

where the damask rose darkens   into an orphaned
kitten, you   spread moonshine   on her hip-arc
teeth new   as snow   gloveless falconer
outside   a church   named   *christabel,*
butter   to cauterize   the last of sirloin
to witness   breaking   a sparrow taunting
its cold bones   into a glass   window as you
compass   the parting of her   amaryllis-cave
your fingers   are now   fluent   in the tarot
of water;   its scent of   cinnamon and psalms
and these miniature   tyrannies   where touch
must come   contoured   with language,   where
the heart can't be   sketched back   into its own

black   horse

Godbot

I am dithering to ax the cleverness
of every slick Freudian homonym.

Bolting

the bushel of babysteps from where
I constellate my trauma in tinsel

of prophetic psychosis. Unabridged, lesson
won't suffice as a placeholder for lessen.

The animal apostrophe of my body can't
punctuate any dirty marble's schisms.

When I turn the bathtub into a cheap clinic,
I let the razorwords cumber all flashbacks.

A shamanic red

limning my wrist with its continued phlogiston -
my heartbeat graphic and pregnant like a hunted marsupial.

The Valium Bride

i
you are the mangled alarm clock inside the rubble : hours leeched to your hamstrings like a jinx of scorpions. you keep ringing with a hiccup of omens.

ii
winter is my stillborn haiku. an alembic parnassus. a casket wired to the cleft in the revolver. a new cosmos shuffling through its syllabus of bitter gravity inside the iota.

iii
someone will hold your hands with the seasoned kindness of a blind rromany seamstress. someone will tell you your freckles are a fresco of unstitched copper sequins dancing on a damp floor.

iv
when you disappear from their lives, most people will remember you like an extinct language : a strange sleight of tongue; a loss wrapped in lingua obscura.
a silent genocide of syntax.

v
heart like a black pentagram carved into the waist of a coral reef.

vi
my medicated arteries run helter-skelter hell tides like the london underground. in my backpack a clandestine stockpile of psychosis pills; a burgled kaleidoscope of kites. *intente volar* : untranslated skies.

vii
a sunday in may you penciled a wanderlust inside the alcove of your arm as though the calendar of your childhood was an atlas of the spice road. you touched the rain with fingers camouflaged in the crushed turmeric of the indian sun. thereafter, all the purgatories cinched to your heels smell like burned cinnamon and revolving doors.

vii
the world is an impacted third molar in need of extraction. you are a small globule of novocain.

viii

the drugs raised you to the status of the lankiest eucalyptus. an army of beetles marched the first koan on your atrophied husk. you fell like the thinnest strand of lightning.

ix

some homes are like the brief pain of papercuts.

x

show me whom you haunt and i will show you how you many times you will need to die.

grrrls

girls with bodies pronounced like explicit quasars. girls with nails, a cloister of hyenas soliciting the ebony prairie out of its colonial pitfalls. girls with dreams paling to anemia. girls with aspens knitted into their fingerprints. girls with guns gardened beneath their tongues. girls with bellybuttons of peeled almonds. girls with breasts like an unspent molotov cocktail. girls with honeycomb hips; terra cotta urns pockmarked. girls with dignity the color of snow-kissed fossils.

girls gone bondage *kawaii* in the digital amphitheater.

girls with hair like graven wicker baskets.
girls with hair like a tonic of seaweed.
girls with hair like a hammered cassette tape.

girls who dipped their twilight in saké. girls who nibbled your earlobes as though it was smoked crabmeat. girls who turned your heart into a chessboard. girls who sped past you in the red-hot miasma of havana black markets. girls with veins beetling from the featherweight fabric of their skin like an arson of bass-lines. girls who play snakes and ladders with their bruises. girls hiding mirrors inside the shallow grave of the smallest starling. girls with bellies writhing as though a wasp's nest.
girls deserted on an inter-state highway in an exile of cherry pits. girls teething against a campfire of daggers.
girls shattered into sibyls; a thin crust geometry guarding the mosaic. girls dying in matinee prints.
girls moving silently inside the shadow of a thread; a gray train speedballing on 5 layers of soi, dancing its junket of dust, pollinating the dusk.

Garganta Rroma

For my Indian, Afghan and Rroma lineages

x

Tantra me a beast. So golden in my fuckability.
Shamed into a river, I am the occupation
of God. Wet sand, wafered cinnamon – apples and
razors in the wake of new hounds. The heat on my
tongue is a spice the sun spat out. Cleopatra's asp
rosaried for the rroma in my roots. My eyes diamond
the blackest jinx. Blacker than a skull boat
tattooed with its own dog-collared kindling.
Look at me: my splayed melusine of *babystealer* blue.
I am bodied from such shameless cosmology -
You couldn't tell whether it was a seashell or
a quicksand that oh-so quietly swallowed you.

Mira as Garganta Rroma

i

Mira, I am complicit in my beheading. Persephone in the streets. Hecate in the sheets. My navel is lined with the musk of *Unwantedness*. You murmur that my eyes are an incantation icebound in time - the snake-hooded Adam's apple of a low Prophet. This city inked itself from an alphabet of crows. You quiz me about the cobra gypsies, the bathtub gin, the calligraphy of myrrh in my hair. The first girl who jumps has already chanted her legs into hemp ropes. Blood thickened to eschatology. My homeland is time's amnesia, a schizophrenic signature – a pessary, atavistic blot . You can italicize this lockjaw of wander, the sieved flashbacks of a wasteland I hooked between my two front teeth. An immigrant's memory is *gurfa* – the amount of water that can be scooped in one hand. A body can't will itself into a fact. So, I am – a honeyed mongrel, a cold and precise animal. I howl and it is thistle. A river you milk to gnosis. Look at the way my eye blows up – pink pinhole, soft belladonna, the rubied gut of lamb we buried in the bomb shelter. Childhood Eyes. Child Who Dies. Shrapnel still shoving cargo under my skin. Synaptic bullfights. Your first cathedral starving its saints between the white light of my bones.

ii

who can fish back the cassiopoeia of those silver
keys from the seismic jewelbox of our mouths?

I swallowed you like I were cloning the canvas of Goya.
Indigo-cloves-Saharan graveyards. Dusk of dark tarot.

The night so full of subtle defeats, its headless quiet tonguing my knee.
I want to call you vino blanco, ropeburn, chopped heads of easter lilies.

This is where the lune of ribs in their malleable heat
bell against each other like a snakebit windchime.

This is where we buried our fathers like lambs in brine.
What is *alone* but a blind child in a very loud house?

All the mothers clutching their pearls and prayerbooks, their arms
veined with chickenwire, their mouths – an enticement for dead birds.

From a drowning

All night the wind shapes ellipses
From the sacrum of sea-husked boats

Water narrows the paisley of its tongue
            As if a persian-blue hyphen

All distance is an emptied hourglass,
An alice universe too luminous in its lie

Men with palms like leatherbound bibles tease
      the weed-cottoned augury of conch-songs

Maghrib is a drooping sonance, a mapless gull
        - a compass breastfed on ambergris

These are the roots I can't be clawed from
 I can't perfume my throat with *Calo*

Just like I can't liquor the blackout of my father's
Suicide. Leaving is cloudless – the sky always

Barefoot, ennobled

                          by its own alizarin calligraphy

Ancestors of rock salt cathedrals
Ancestors of stormchasing caravans

What am I if not splintered phosphorescence?
          A gasp of voltage. Trickled Trout.

The spine of God filigreeing the coral
Cave of my mouth. The chambered echo

Of my heart flowering inwards
             Into a hungry anemone

.

Volver, Dame tu mano

There will be more evenings to fail :
unbuttoned copperpods, a few crinkles

loosening the rose-ringed beaks of waxwings.

Defeather the sky and the carcass of this
dusk is a coffin we haven't nailed shut yet.

Every mother wears the agate omen of
a daughter she could not bury or flame.

Hair lengthened into a worship song -

glory to bone. Its godly quicksilver. Its faint
saudade hummed to a shivering switchblade.

Glory to breath. Ghostless haunting. I tried
to scheme myself into a quieter animal -

flattened moans, iron-kissed hooves.
But the blood plugged in its tightrope

and all I could hear was hunger, sainted,
stretched between the shrines of my teeth.

Oscuridad

i

You speak about growing the most arduous orchids -
vanilla-fonts in a cuneiform of shamrock green,

their pale spellings columned in heather-snow.
The solstice drags out your harvest's gold, their pixie tongues

lighting the room where we are unbarred in the ghost
- swans of *nag champa* smoke, sigils bodied in squid ink.

Your hands abled by mire, my mouth :
an arc of fathomless alizarin.

You promise every forbiddance - the secour of each lovesick
incongruity drawing us out from an abundance of syruped messes.

You lower your boughs into this cockled spate; new flickers
of spoon oars grazing the surface of a loosened pond.

I cauterize your name - summer's first flames limping through
cyclamens and mallow, a mirage tucked under thunder and fire.

A grapevine of holly blue ready to sip their cup from my
apollo's horn. You tilt your head towards this dark earth,

watch each seed slowly gush to its own tender spawning.

ii

consciousness // erose // in its untold wharf
and the way its eigengrau   buoys

the scarceness of everything
i can't pry to a pearl -

give it an opportunity for   missing,
for abridgement that will   construe

the tongue into a tremored   sanguinity
this forbidden emphasis,   mirador tolling

the venise ravel of comber.   i fail
to assimilate into this   usable hollow

this nocturnal torrent
fluent in every version of the glissade

i, of mantis-green riverfonts
i, of abeyant boats

whose body stretches
from this dark into another

like a name hyphenated by the echo
of its own   returning wave

iii

no one comes home when the night is exonerated
in the gimmicks of barred owls.

through a paradox of dole and throe, he must be taught
how to revisit the mink-coy slink of my skin

divorced from the premonitions of a boy yoked
to a bull's eye // the godly falconry of his hands

the way in which he still starves the motives of his bones
as if a new season will venerate the ropeswell of his vines

inside the polysemy of rain. will chew up the blue spruce of every
mountain's breath. will comply with the algorithms of absences.

he unsettles the sheets as if the act of moving is measurement
for the best tense we can stitch ourselves into - his fiction

contrived into earthly madnesses. leaving hoofprints to sear
the locus of every numb lake. the water breaking open

its welcome   asking us - go. unlearn again.

iv

body as a-stone-in-throat, an earthwound
so alluvial, the *eskhara* was dressed

back to its corporeal settlings.
you - in your arsenal - robin egg blue,

chimerical neptune, berry-pith.
depression blue. shark blue.

blue as the rue-veined tinder
of this murder season's breakthrough.

tongue nooked, naked - outblooming
the taunting bones of its corral.

mijo, you must first learn
the colours in their musk'd *garra*.

shoal the mouth with *verd* or *lila* or *grana*.
sting seasalt into the sun's rose and gourd.

gallo rojo still raying the streets,
mouth thinned songwards -

leaving the last of its music
to a marriage of light and silt.

eskhara : ancient greek – hearth (origin of the word
"scar" especially in context to
"scar tissue".)

verd/lila/grana – green/lilac/red in Spanish.

gallo rojo – a popular Spanish song

v

dear leaf of god, i am your weather of limerence, of fogs
ribbed in mollusk-stencils. the sleep of a flower mantis

costumed in an orchid-trap. empiric organ, blissful gluttony.
a strand of dew to milden this settling of mummery.

bare me to your horned tang, its untenable calando.
the mandible snapping out from its own gushing cave.

in us, the bourne of a thing, its perpetual outwardness. your
lineament mortised to my roost. your tendrils all snow-n-gunpowder,

every tuft, each tallow - crimson narcotic, routes of red-winged dandelion.
give me my promised cleaving : the primrose and its winding serpent.

our bodies and their sundered economies, subtle forgeries. the way you
say *zahara* - mouth still white-gold from the heat of your own seed.

how the ache must travel from shin to knuckle.
how darling the way i lope and muddle in your lucid direction

vi

last night, my father came back as a boatman's aubade
slinking its feet in a lily-jeweled monastery for new minnows .

his voice tenderly harrowing the abeyance of an opaque dream,
the water quartered to a four-way dialogue of broken chords.

in a courtyard of plantains, the ghost always reifies itself
in the shape of two peacocks; one perched atop the other;

twin beds of spooked bijou; each preen handwritten in phthalo blue.
dusk's mussed-up sheaves curl for hours into the straw-plaited bylanes

of our old neighborhood. its winter inviolable under the amnesty of
incense oil and coal-hazed bakeries. its foreign voices tearing up

the riverside in a babel of muscle and pining. in its numbing depths
my father's body flattening its voluted hibiscus - a flowering tea,

memory   convulsing

its red seeds into the carnal soil. the skylarks hovering over
the embankment in a rearrangement of astrology charts.

Death Valley - V

The day I left, your hands floated away like kite wings. The moon broke over Devil's golfcourse in a prolonged lysis, mirroring the private eclipse of our chemistry. I felt the rainwater puddle within the smallest chasms in my consciousness. Earlier, I had studied the crackling science of air trapped into salt, whole of the earth broken up in the tiniest pencil-points of a child's chewed up rage. *This is you,* I confessed to the giddy faces of panamint daisies expanding their once-in-20-years empire of superbloom behind the Needle's arch. The dried up riverbed opened like a cut lip; red with its dowry of secrets, green with the deathless trauma. My body was still slanging its zero-sum game with a medicated routine. At the top of the butte, you were no larger than a housefly, a flitting murmur before silence slapped loss back into the landscape. I am gifted with pessimism. I always predict the wrong things right. That night, us, sleeping in the back of your car like two whales knotted into one shrimp-sized fishing net, I woke up twice to see the stars giggling above us as if a playground full of kids before they learn words like divorce or type 2 diabetes. With your heartbeat in my hand, I knew I would have to start learning a new language to welcome something equally brutal taking shape to balance the accident of *this:* an unspoken beautiful, a bridge between *for me to but not mine.*

Bone

He watched himself shatter - a boy poured out like light whispering through the open mouth of a keyhole, a cold stone against the mosque's rose window, a scatter of metallic salts. Damascus raveled in layers of oxblood silk.

The song's bombed silhouette - *a boat. a body. a border.*

In a house abbreviated by twilight, loosened threads of nightshade spasm and curve into a shadow theater of ghosts. The first bird unsettles the wet bamboo of lawn chairs like a pint-sized spaceship - its wings still sunlit with a trodden wildness.

Outside, the rooftops had wintered in a dream-blur of casablanca lilies; the muezzin's baritone cutting through coughs of low clouds.

I carry on me the hips of *harappan* urns, perigee moons dug out from the chest of a sleeping Indus. A neck as tenuous as a terracotta figurine. This tongue's blessed votive. This stamped cunt of vermilion clay.

All my mongrel organs – wet and muzzled.

Under the oilcloth of cassia flowers, our women shell pistachios, blade the gingerroot, crush betel nuts with a blunt laughter.

Our bodies are as wanted as fake passports in a shoreless country. Our bodies are as hated as a boatful of foreign names.

They promise to hook you up by the question mark of your own rib. Promise you the sinking continents of waterlogged lungs; a new city afloat in your own blood's unflagging, tidal panic.

They hose rifle butts with mustard oil. They continue to promise you the horror of survival.

In the desert, girls gnawed the map like wolves suckling on buffalo bones.

The last soldier asked a one-eyed tea seller: *why do boys here blow up like a battalion of old bottle rockets?*

Last night they were scraping for a trail of tendons, bone fragments shuffled like cowrie shells before the vultures ascended for alms.

In a dream, I can revise my bruise as a body full of sleep and and quiet certainties.

I believe it is easier to break when you have never hoped to be whole.

éphémère

At first, the egress and its sodden nectary - I hinder
his light down to each incalculable trough. It stipples, then
cottons the blue lace blur of his face, moils and murmurs -
quincena

\+

Nowhere has the world lasted longer for me
than in a phonecall's shuddered radius, a new bar
-reling of tenses : and now my father *went, did, was*

\+

That farness, its fitted falcon / its beak's sermoned pellet
Marshrains fraying the gossan of our eulogies to powdered glass

\+

Judith fated God as the name for what opposes Myth
Then him: Hierophant carved from the moan of a mountain
Then I: his bone's bastard font, his body black-boxed, unbaptised

\+

He was the purple brogue of Veronica and phlox
Before the herbaceous gall, before the moth-lick of a milky sap
In pale stillness, each bee-prong praying for a common descent

\+

Morning / torn syllables of salt-broken seaweed
After / a wave's demotic shell, every oyster in her illegible Eros,
each creviced crab, an abandoned harvest -

My sonder
His staying

+

The sea from here is just distance licking its own
cinereal abscess. All hiss and pang, a tongue slid in
between speech and its skein. The grey scrape of its talons,
its plenary recoil as long as Time's own ravening spine

+

To earn his memory back from my own jouissance
Finger by finger kissing the whole rope: *goodbye*

Left of Azul

i

Forgiveness extinguishes its canaries on the damp coal of badly tutored tongues. Another day, another erudition that desires to knife out the second "r" from Rroma. Cue : Pharrijmos, slurred and schismed, as in another Us cut up from the root, as in genocide, as in the way this ancestry lullabies my body through its dysthymia. At midnight, the legerdemain of his eyelash breaches the cartomancy of my cheekbone – (t)his whiteness of being - axiomatic and unpurposed. I am thinking about my grandmother's hair falling like sheaves of phosphor, a mouthful of snow in the Hindkush, ندروخ هصغ (ghosseh khordan); to eat sorrow. To eat it wild. Now, I have mouthfuls of dark chants, words crawling about the altar of my tongue like torched wood-ants. This reluctance to effervesce for him, to peal and pour like a heartdeep blunder. To let his voice whistle through me as a prelude to a storm. I know that the oldest hungers in my skin must fold in a straight line. Every kiss sparks another sun to pray for me. Every aura is verduous with its own worm-hedged leafing. My eyes now rich with Tahoe and its stars. The wound of his name slowly split between woman and war.

ii

Darwish augured our ivy-crawl on the stone wall of a cave - *"I will take this gazelle from its flock and gore myself with it."* I am the weakest machete of my flock. The Sufi eulogizes His heart as the squirrel of Light, a brief warmth flitting against our eyes through inventories of Otherwheres. My father – a fire that flowered me into an endless dance. All this music and my feet still locked in his shoes. These bones are heavy with a romani tiredness. Tiredness with its ex-cathedra blueprints. Tiredness who kisses my ankles with a practiced luxury. Tiredness with its gilt-lipped language of masked leafhoppers and medallion-yellow birds refusing the whole length of lake-air. Tiredness is my inherited dialect. Language, says Paz, is *"time portioned as body."* If time would swallow us back, we'd perhaps raise our fathers to be something other than wind howling through revolving doors.

iii

The science I quiz annotates for me the viper-wreathed pathways of pain. Still fails to explain why my left eye blurs an omen when the ablution of depression pours into me like rosewater in bleach bottles. My grandmother taught me the remedy of flowers; gorse and honeysuckle; song and bezoar. Her desultory prophet remains ungrasped. A room so duty-bound to the redeemer. A tongue limned with its own tameless perdition. Her palm hardening into its own illegible hollow. On the bevel of my backbone, the sun has printed its sleepless mirages. *Falak*. Firmament. These alterities are luminescent in me - fishing villages, honeycombed skyscrapers, footlights encoded like a *tasbih* of collected teeth. If I now say I love you, I probably mean a synapse in shape of a knife. I probably mean the way wind knocks hardest on gutted roofs. I mean the way trees set themselves on fire just to meet the smallest possibility of rain.

Author's Bio

Scherezade Siobhan is an award-winning Indo-Rroma writer, psychologist and community catalyst who founded and runs The Talking Compass— a therapeutic space dedicated to providing counseling services and decolonizing mental health care. She is the author of three books, including *Bone Tongue* (Thought Catalog, 2015), *Father, Husband* (Salopress, 2016) and *The Bluest Kali* (Lithic Press, 2018). Her work has been featured or is forthcoming in *Medium, Berfrois, Feministing, DIAGRAM, Rattle, Jubilat, DATABLEED, Nat Brut,* and *Winter Tangerine*, among others. She is the creator and curator of The Mira Project— a global dialogue against street harassment, gendered violence and in support of women's mental health. She has performed and lectured across the world; her poems and essays are taught at psychology and creative writing courses in various parts of the world.